I Live Here Too
By Wanda Gray

Book Design, Illustrations & Photography by Pat Lee

Humanics Limited
881 Peachtree St., N. E.
Suite 112
Atlanta, Georgia 30309

PRINTED IN THE UNITED STATES OF AMERICA

ISBN 0-89334-013-8

CONTENT

Chapter 1

You Are One of a Kind

If you could see the earth from a distance, as
a spaceman might, you would see billions of people
living here, in deserts, on mountain tops, in jungles, by
the sea, and all the places in between. You would find them
in huge cities, often stacked one on top of the other in great
apartment complexes. You'd see people in small towns
and villages, and sometimes alone, living away
from all other people.

Coming closer, you would notice many, many different kinds of people--men, women, and children of varied colors and physical appearance. You would find people who can buy every commercial thing they want, others who live comfortably, and many more who go to bed hungry and get up hungry. You'd see sick people and well people, rich and poor, old and young, fat and thin, happy and sad.

You would see people working at thousands of jobs and occupations: mothers and fathers, doctors and lawyers, bankers, factory workers, farmers and movie stars, missionaries, athletes, artists, dancers, musicians and plumbers ———— and too many more to name.

Some people you'd see at war, or in prisons, or in hospitals, and others moving around freely and peacefully. You would see people dying and others being born. If you could see the earth from a distance, sooner or later you would probably see every possible thing people are capable of doing.

3

But you are not a spaceman.
You live here, too.

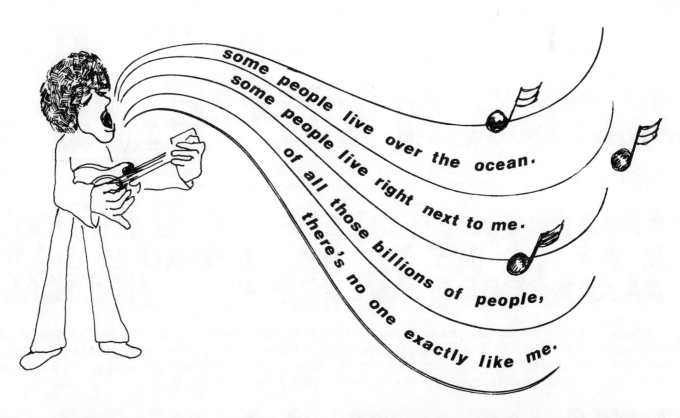

some people live over the ocean.
some people live right next to me.
of all those billions of people,
there's no one exactly like me.

But you are not a spaceman. You live here, too. And you already know something about the differences in people. You may also know, of all the billions of people alive, you are the only one who is exactly you.

You are somewhat like all the other people. A scientist could identify you as a member of Homo Sapiens, the scientific name for people. You are a warm blooded mammal who stands and walks upright and who has a complex nervous and intelligence system. You also have a personality, which helps make you different from every other person.

There are other people who might fit into some of the same categories as you, such as young, student, happy or sad, boy or girl, American, but none of them is exactly like you. You are one of a kind.

You have your own unique way of seeing, hearing, talking, and putting ideas together. You are the only one who can ever really know all your feelings, characteristics and talents—even you may never know them all! You can explore and develop them throughout your life, to become the person you want to be, or you can ignore them. Then they will be lost to the world forever, for there will never be another you!

How can you grow toward being all you can?
You've already started, of course, because you were growing and
changing even before you were born, and that was about a dozen years
ago. But a good way to continue is to learn everything you can about yourself
and to learn as much as you can about the people around you. It will also help to
remember that your intelligence, nervous system, and personality make it possible for
you to change things around you, what you do, the way you think---you can even change
some things about your body. As the only living you in the world, the kind of person you are
is mostly up to you.

JOURNAL

GETTING TO KNOW YOU

Today, make yourself a journal to keep a record of who you are, what you think, and how you grow. You can write anything you like in your journal, and you will also be given some assignments to put in it. Make a cover that says something about yourself, or use your favorite colors, or cut pictures from magazines showing things you like. Whatever you do, make it yours.

For the first pages of your journal, write:

1. Six things that describe you

    I am.......

2. Ten things you like or like to do

    I like........

3. Four things you would like to do, if you could

    I would like to......

4. Three words that you would like people to say about you

    I would like people to say that.....

5. Three words that tell how you treat other people

    I treat other people.....

6. Three words that tell how you want other people to treat you.

    I want other people to be.....

7. Write one thing you would like to change about yourself

    I would like to change.....

8. Write two things you are proud of having done

    I am proud that I.....

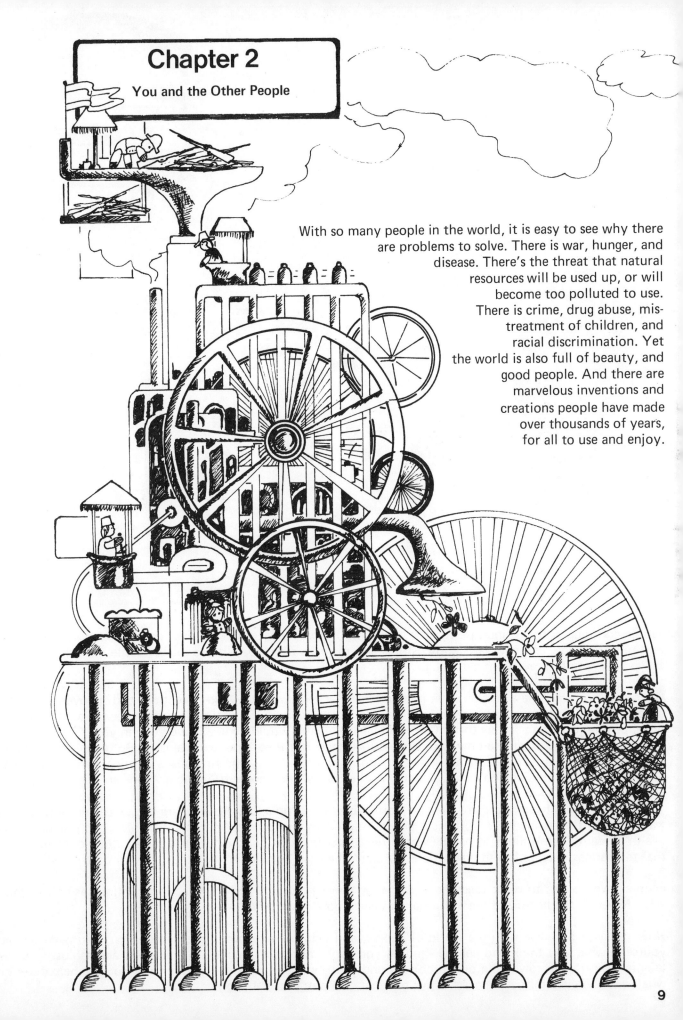

Chapter 2

You and the Other People

With so many people in the world, it is easy to see why there are problems to solve. There is war, hunger, and disease. There's the threat that natural resources will be used up, or will become too polluted to use. There is crime, drug abuse, mistreatment of children, and racial discrimination. Yet the world is also full of beauty, and good people. And there are marvelous inventions and creations people have made over thousands of years, for all to use and enjoy.

People continually try to increase what is good and decrease what is destructive. That's why discoveries and inventions are made, and why laws and customs and manners develop. With so many people, there have to be organized ways to help everyone get along.

Of course, not everyone agrees on what is good and what is destructive. Also, inventions and discoveries are sometimes misused, and laws, customs, and manners don't always work. Sometimes they are inappropriate and sometimes people just don't follow them. Can you imagine what it would be like if everyone in your class tried to get into a telephone booth at one time, to make a call? Chaos! Yet there's no law against it. But people have 'survival sense', or respectful manners, or both, so they don't all crowd into one tiny space at once, and risk squashing one another to death. Even on a crowded bus, you'll usually find people trying to give one another room.

Think what would happen if there were no traffic laws, and people just drove where and when and how fast they wanted to at the moment. What if most people refused to take the vaccinations available, or to practice known health precautions? Millions of people would die of smallpox or polio or other diseases. But would anyone say that telephones, cars, or health precautions are bad? They can be misused. Are they good or destructive?

People have learned to work together to use what they know, and perhaps that will continue as new problems arise. Never, in the history of the world, has this been more important.

How can you best live with the world of people, and help solve common problems? First, you need to know yourself---what you think and believe---and all you can about other people. If you know and can use your own talents, you usually solve your own problems, and contribute to solutions for everyone. You can help determine what laws and customs people need to live together, the way you want to live.

A good way to know more about yourself and other people is to work in a small group. That way, as you share your thoughts and feelings, you begin to see how each person in the group is alike in some ways and different in others. You will see that you really **are** unique, but it may make you feel good to find other people worry, get scared, feel angry and mean, or feel happy and successful, just the way you do.

WORKING IN GROUPS — You've already spent a lot of time in groups. In fact, by the time you're 11 or 12, you've spent several **years** in groups. At home, you're in a group called family. At school, you're in a class, or maybe several classes. You may also go to a church, or belong to a club or organization, such as Scouts, or 4—H. Or maybe you play an instrument in a band, or belong to a dance group, or share some other interest or hobby in a club. Sometimes it may seem the only time you're alone is when you're asleep.

Yet you **do** find some time when you're alone, just with your self. You read, or play a game alone, or practice piano. Maybe you do some chore, like washing dishes, or delivering papers, or cleaning your room. Then you can think, and make plans, and have dreams. Sometimes you think about yourself,and sometimes you think about the other people you know, and how you are getting along with them.

Often you may feel lost and alone, even when you are with a group of familiar people. You feel you are not important, and if you were not there nobody would notice. Most people feel that way now and then. What complicated animals people are---lonely in a group, or 'with' other people when alone. You are not stuck in the present. With your brain and feelings and imagination, you can go into the past or the future with ease.

Although you have been **you** your entire life, have spent several years in groups, and have studied such subjects as English, math, history, and geography, you probably have never studied **people**. Who are you, really? What makes you special? What is it like, living in your own skin, alone? What is it like, living with other people? Who are all these homo sapiens living on the planet Earth in the last half of the 20th century? As you grow, you'll probably find a way to say proudly to each other person, 'I live here, too.'

11

GROUP ACTION

Divide your class into groups of four or five people each. Let one be a recorder in each group. The recorder will write individual and group ideas to share later with the entire class. After your discussion, put the records on the wall, for everybody to see and talk about.

1. Quickly list all the groups you can to which someone in your small group belongs. (Family, Scouts, etc.) Take four minutes for this.

2. Quickly list activities people in your group do when alone. Four minutes.

3. List five things you, as a group, are proud that people have accomplished in the world. Take two minutes.

4. List five things you think need to be changed or improved. Two minutes.

5. List ways you think you can help make these changes or improvements. Four minutes.

6. Make at least one, or not more than four, rules that would make living together easier, if everyone followed your rules. Five minutes.

Now share your group's thinking with the entire class.

JOURNAL

Today, in your journal, write about what you do when you are alone. Then make a schedule of a 'typical day' for you, to see how much time you spend in groups. (Make this in the shape of a clock, if you like.) Can you think of a time when you were in a group, but felt left out or lonely? You may want to write about it in your journal.

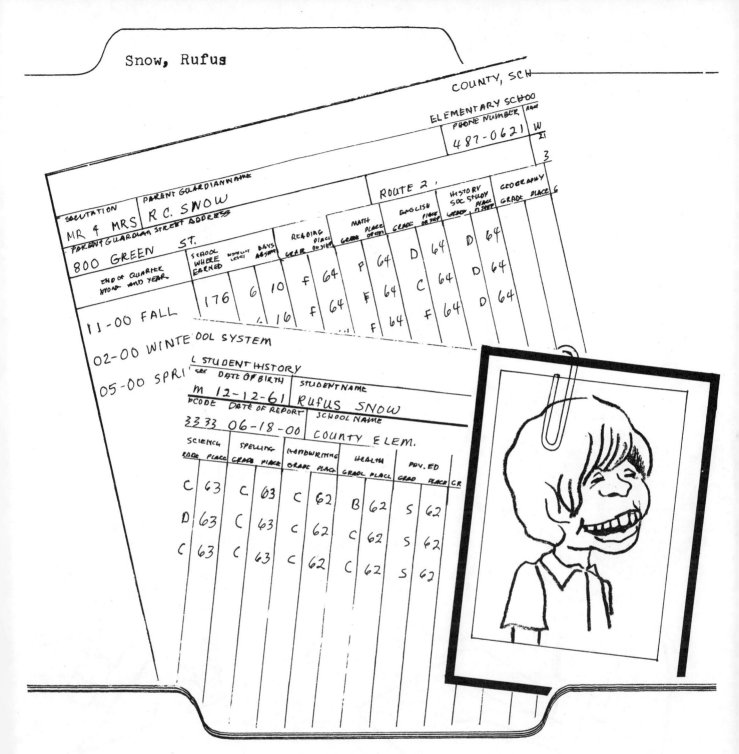

Chapter 3

Look At One Person: Rufus, A Case Study

You have taken a quick look at yourself and a quick look at the world. Now, before you start learning more about yourself and the others in your class, get some practice studying people by trying to help Rufus. You will be his advisor, and you want to help him be happier and more successful at school. You have to be a good detective to do this.

Teachers, counselors, and other advisors are often a lot like detectives, too. They gather little bits of information wherever they can and put them together, so they can help someone solve a particular problem. Of course, nobody can really solve another person's problems---you have to do that yourself---but sometimes outside advice is very helpful. Rufus has a lot of problems and needs help. See what you can find out about him, then give the best advice you can.

Rufus is in the sixth grade. He doesn't like school very much, and is late or absent as often as he can find a believeable excuse. When he comes into class, he usually breaks up whatever is going on by asking what is happening, trying to find his books, getting paper and pencils, and sometimes by saying the assignment is silly or stupid.

When this happens, some of the other kids stop working, too, or they agree with Rufus, and say, 'Yeah, this **is** stupid,' or 'Why do we have to do something that even Rufus knows is silly!' Other classmates just **ignore** him, but that is hard to do, with all the **disturbance.**

The teacher tries to help him get started with his work, but Rufus just laughs and starts when he gets good and ready. Sometimes he does what the teacher asks, but sometimes he does his work, then tears it up and throws it on the floor. Sometimes he puts his head on his desk and goes to sleep, and everybody is relieved.

14

Rufus is failing almost every subject, although he made average grades up until this year. He certainly does not want to be in the sixth grade again, but he seems headed for failure. Why is Rufus behaving this way? Can you help him?

HELP FOR RUFUS — As a class, plan your strategy for advising Rufus. List whatever reasons you can for his behavior. What else do you need to know? How will you find out? If you were in Rufus's class, could you see some ways to help him? At this point, what is your advice?

MORE INFORMATION — Rufus's teacher knows he is having trouble. He knows that a person has to like himself and feel capable before he can do good work and get along well with others, and he thinks Rufus does not feel this way about himself. He can't seem to help Rufus much, though, so he turns his case over to a counselor.

The counselor did some detective work. She talked to Rufus, his parents, and some of his friends. She found that Rufus had a job after school. In fact, he had several jobs. He was newspaper delivery boy every day. Then he mowed grass around the neighborhood, and did other jobs, too, such as taking care of people's pets when they were away, or watering their plants, or babysitting. The people who hired Rufus thought he was very responsible and did good work.

Rufus also had three younger brothers and was expected to do many chores at home. Both his mother and father went to work every day, and Rufus was in charge until they came home at 5:30.

Rufus told the counselor he spent all his spare time inventing things. (This was the first time at school anyone ever asked Rufus what he really liked to do.) He said he almost never got to invent or build things at school, which was what he enjoyed most and was good at doing.

The counselor gave Rufus some tests and found that he was average in reading and math, even though he was failing both these subjects in school. Rufus said he invented things by 'just trying them out and watching what works and what doesn't.'

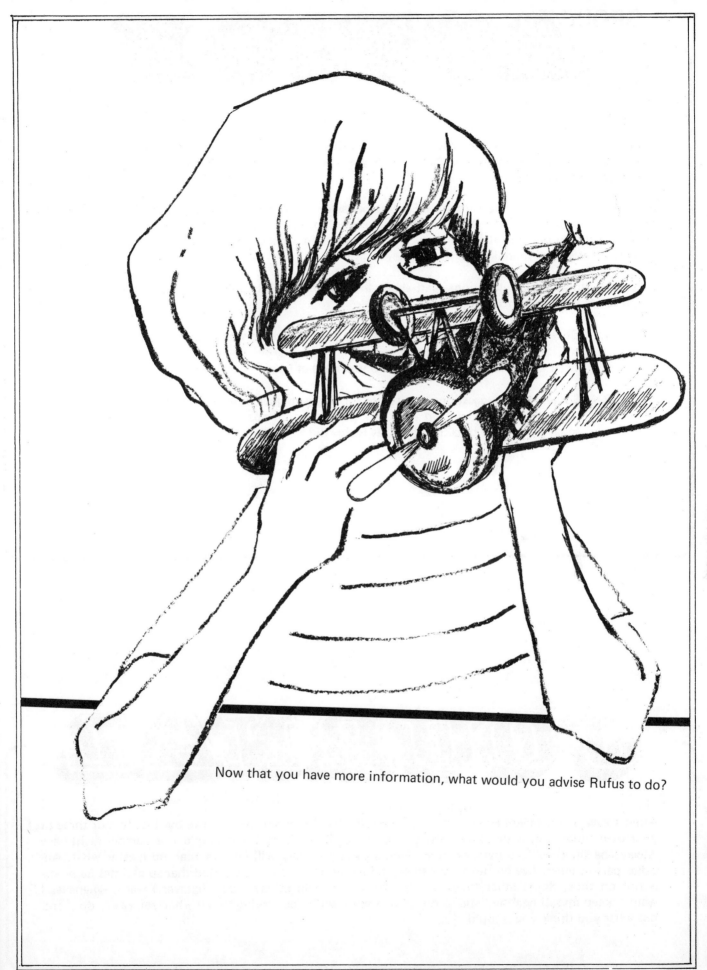

Now that you have more information, what would you advise Rufus to do?

GROUP ACTION

Break into small groups to plan your advice for Rufus. Look back at the suggestions the whole class made. Now that you know more, decide what you want to add or take away. Let one person in each group write the suggestions.

Be sure you consider what Rufus DOES (his behavior) before you decide what and how he should change. For instance, he is often late or misses school, he goes to sleep in class, he sometimes tears up his work, and so on. But at home he works hard and often makes inventions. Can you help him find ways to be at school more like he is at home?

After you finish your suggestions, and share them with the class, take a few more minutes in your group to let each person talk briefly about:

1. Do you think you behave differently at home from the way you do at school?

2. What chores and responsibilities do you have at home?

3. Some of the suggestions you wrote for Rufus might be simply a matter of good manners, such as being on time. Do you think people should obey such rules, even if they have personal reasons for breaking them, as Rufus did?

JOURNAL

Almost everybody makes some 'rules' for himself, that he or she tries to live by. List two or three of your own 'rules' and write about how you try to abide by them. For example, one person might have 'always be on time' as a personal rule. Such a person usually will be punctual, no matter what. Another person might live by 'take your time, and enjoy what you do' and find that sometimes he or she is not on time. Some other 'rules' are 'be friendly,' 'help others,' 'do whatever I want, whenever I want,' 'keep myself healthy,' and so on. Write your own 'rules,' trying to tell what you really do, and not what you think you 'should' do.

Chapter 4

Your Own Case Studies

When you were in a group, working on Rufus's case, did you learn anything new about yourself and other people in the group? You may begin to see that you don't behave the same way in every group, just as Rufus didn't behave the same way at home and at school.

In some groups you may be a leader and in others, a follower. You may talk a lot in one, and be quiet in another. This is usually influenced by how you feel, how much you know about the subject you are working on, and the other people in your group. But whatever you do at a particular time, it is wise to remember that your actions influence everyone around you, just as their actions influence you. Did you know that? Remember how Rufus disrupted his class, and some people agreed with him and others tried to ignore him? That couldn't happen if he had had no influence.

Look around you.

Who is in your class? Probably you see a few friends you know very well, some you know less well and perhaps feel less friendly toward, and a few you hardly know at all. You, and each person in your class, have case histories just as Rufus did---although you probably don't have as many problems. Could you be a detective, as Rufus's counselor was, and write a case study about another person in your class?

People usually tell about themselves only to those they trust, and trust is a basic part of friendship. Can you be trusted? Do you trust every other person in your class? If you do, you are very lucky. But once everyone begins to know and understand everyone else, usually the entire group can be trusted. Today, take the time to get to know other people in your class. Each person will write a brief case study of one other person, and each will have a case study written about him or her.

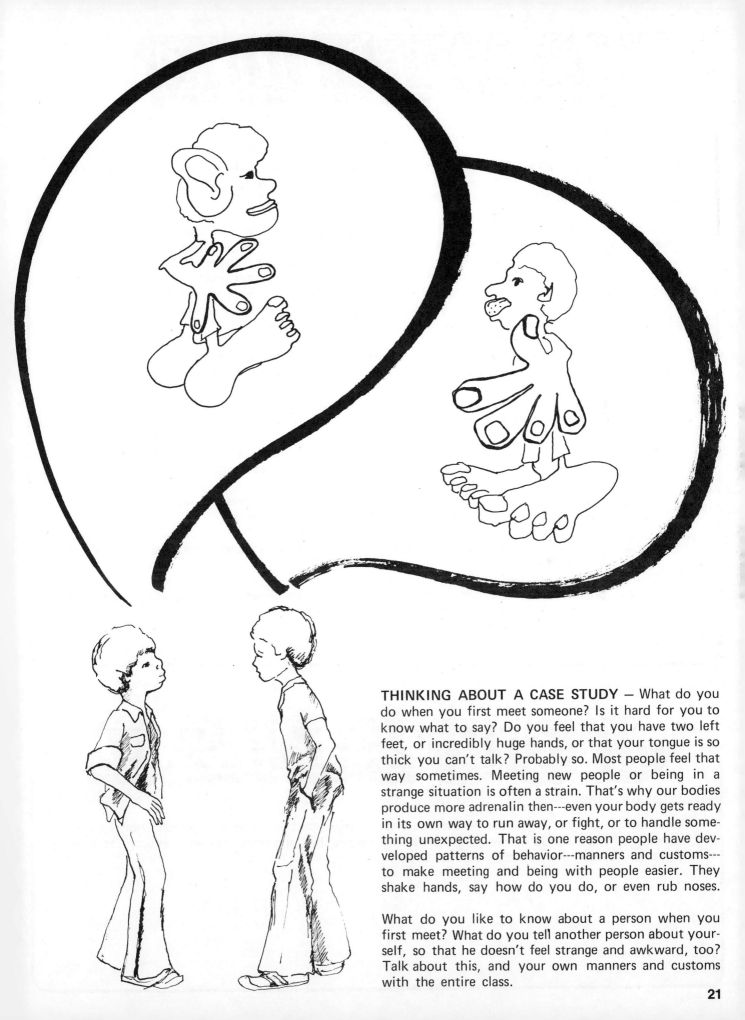

THINKING ABOUT A CASE STUDY — What do you do when you first meet someone? Is it hard for you to know what to say? Do you feel that you have two left feet, or incredibly huge hands, or that your tongue is so thick you can't talk? Probably so. Most people feel that way sometimes. Meeting new people or being in a strange situation is often a strain. That's why our bodies produce more adrenalin then---even your body gets ready in its own way to run away, or fight, or to handle something unexpected. That is one reason people have developed patterns of behavior---manners and customs---to make meeting and being with people easier. They shake hands, say how do you do, or even rub noses.

What do you like to know about a person when you first meet? What do you tell another person about yourself, so that he doesn't feel strange and awkward, too? Talk about this, and your own manners and customs with the entire class.

GROUP ACTION

Now divide into groups of two. Each person will later introduce his partner to the entire group. You will write a case study of your partner to use when you introduce him or her, just as he or she will write a case study about you, and introduce you to the class.

Some questions you might consider asking are: What is your favorite food? What do you do after school? Have you ever had a broken bone or a severe illness? When? How did it happen? Do you have brothers and sisters? Have you lived any other place? What is your favorite activity at school? At home? What is something most people don't know about you that you don't mind their knowing? What is your favorite sport? What foods do you like? Do you know what you want to be when you grow up? Where were you born? Did you like first grade? Try to find out as much about the other person as you can. Be a good detective.

When you introduce one another, use a tape recorder if you can. You might want to listen to these tapes again, to hear how you sound on tape, or to hear again what someone else said about you.

After you introduce each other, you might want to practice some ways that make meeting people easier, by role playing. Here are some situations you can role play.

1. The Queen of England is coming to visit you because you are a famous artist and she likes your work. You introduce her to your two best friends, a scientist and a writer.

2. You are the host on a T V talk show. Your guests are an actress, a plumber, and a doctor. You have to introduce them to each other and to the audience.

3. You are at a ballgame with your father, when you meet a friend from school who is with his parents.

4. Have several people, or even the entire class, role play a party. Each person takes on a role of his own choosing, introduces himself and is introduced to other people. Choose two or three hosts and hostesses.

JOURNAL

What famous person would you most like to meet? Imagine that you meet that person. Describe your meeting, who the person is, why you want to meet him or her, and what the two of you say. How do you think meeting this person would affect you?

Chapter 5

As Others see you

You may have been surprised when you were being interviewed for your case study to find that others don't always see you the way you see yourself.

Do you ever wonder if you truly know yourself? Or what other people are **really** thinking when you say or do something? Probably all people do.

One of the best reasons for learning about yourself in a small group is to get other people's views. But remember, the purpose of sharing in your group is to **help** each other, so try to be honest and helpful with your comments, without hurting the other person's feelings.

After all, you probably are not going to change much if someone yells at you, 'I think it's disgusting, the way you always complain!' But you might change if the same person said, 'You're really fun to work with when you're happy, but when you complain it makes things hard for all of us. I wish you were your happy self more of the time.'

An effective rule to remember in your group is: Don't attack people; help them. Learn to say what you have to say in such a way that the other person can **use** your information. You also have to decide **when** you can be helpful, and when it's best not to interfere.

You may be afraid or shy about saying what you think or doing what you feel sometimes, because of what other people may be thinking. That can be good, if what you want to do is hit or hurt another person because you're angry or frustrated. But you've probably learned that that is one of the times when it is best **not** to do what you feel like doing.

Other times, being afraid of what people think is not such a good thing. Maybe you see somebody crying or in trouble and you think you could comfort him or help him out. But then you become afraid that he'll think you are meddling, if you try to help. So you stand by, or even ignore what is happening.

Almost everyday in the newspapers you can find stories of people being robbed on the street, or mugged, or even killed in full view of other people. Afterwards, when interviewed, the witnesses say they 'were afraid of becoming involved.' Do you think these people are afraid, physically, or are they afraid of what other people will think of them?

Usually people are happy to have help, whether it is verbal, as when you give your opinion, or physical, as in stopping someone from hurting another. You probably feel kindly toward people who help you, too. It is a good idea to care more about what you think of yourself than about what others think, although that is often hard to do? What do you think about this?

GROUP ACTION

Make the following continuum for the whole class on the chalkboard. (A continuum is a long line, showing opposite extremes and a midpoint.)

Involved Inez   Middle Marvin   Fearful Freddie

Involved Inez becomes involved in everything she hears about or sees, from killing baby seals and littering in the park to stopping arguments between friends. She says she wants to give all the help she can, and no matter what anyone thinks, she will go to the rescue when she learns about a problem.

Fearful Freddie is afraid to become involved in anything. He thinks people will laugh at him if he shows he cares, or that if he interrupts a fight the fighters will turn on him. His motto is, 'let the problems solve themselves, as long as I am left alone.'

Middle Marvin becomes involved when he thinks he can really help someone who wants help, but if there is anyone else to do the job, he goes on about his business.

Now, let each person in the class draw a line on the continuum and place his name on it, showing whether he is closer to Involved Inez, Fearful Freddie, or Middle Marvin. Talk about your positions.

Divide into small groups and let each person talk for a minute or two about these questions:

1. Have you ever been in trouble when no one came to your aid? (For instance, have you lost your lunch money, or bus fare, or been lost, or bullied by older kids?) What did you do? How did you feel?

2. Have you ever helped anyone in trouble? What did you do? Were you scared? Is it easier to help your friends than people you don't know?

3. Decide, as a group, what you would do if you saw a 16-year-old girl taking a 7-year-old boy's lunch money. Write your solution down and read it to the entire class later.

4. Take turns being 'it' while every person in the group tells one thing he really likes about 'it.'

JOURNAL

Today, write about a time when you helped someone in trouble. Then write another paragraph about what you would like people to think of you. Third, think of someone you admire in your class, and write what you like about that person. Does the person know that you admire him? You may want to tell him some of the things you like about him.

Chapter 6

Know How You Feel

Although all people have feelings, we may not have them in the same ways. We become angry for different reasons, and we show anger in varied ways. But we all feel angry at one time or another. We don't feel happy about the same things, but we all know what it is to feel happy. We all feel like hitting or hurting at some time, and we have all felt generous, giving, and kind.

Usually we separate our feelings into two groups, 'good' feelings and 'bad' feelings, and we all have some of both. Usually we feel proud of our 'good' feelings and guilty about our 'bad' feelings. We try to hide the 'bad' ones. We only want to admit those everyone else will accept and admire.

The best way to know and work with your own feelings is to admit both, and to remember that a feeling, by itself, is neither good **nor** bad. It's what you **do** to express your feelings that counts. For instance, if you become angry enough to hit someone, but you play volleyball and hit the ball hard instead, was your feeling good or bad?

Once you know what your feelings are, and admit them, you can begin to work with them intelligently. You can discourage the ones you don't like, or the ways you express them, and you can develop the ones you can feel good about.

Think for a minute about what you are feeling, right now. Turn to your neighbor and tell him what you would do to express your feelings if you were not in school.

You can see right away that sometimes your feelings and expression are frustrated. If you want to run because you are happy, but you have to sit still at a desk, you will become frustrated if you don't find an **alternative** way to express your happiness---one that allows you to sit still and feel happy.

Frustration makes your immediate feelings harder to handle, so don't feel bad if it slows you down a bit. Finding alternative ways to express your feelings, and learning to wait for an appropriate time to do what you want is often difficult. But it's an important part of becoming mature people. Good Luck!

ANGER

Anger often comes with other feelings, such as the feeling that you have been **treated unjustly.** For instance, you get a paper back from the teacher at school with a poor grade on it. You know you worked very hard on the paper, yet you still got a poor grade. Suddenly you are angry. You think the teacher is a dimwit. (What would you **do**? Would you tear up the paper and throw it on the floor, as Rufus did?)

30

Anger may also come from a feeling of **helplessness.** Here's an example. Angela arrived home from school one day, and found that her three-year-old brother had gotten into her treasure box. He scattered her letters, souvenirs, and jewelry around the room. Some of it was lost and some broken. It was too late to tell him not to do it, or to hide the box, so Angela just felt helpless and angry. You might feel the same way if you came out of school and discovered your bike had been stolen.

If an injustice happens to you and you are helpless to do anything about it or even if you **feel** helpless the result is usually anger. That is why people often feel anger toward those who have authority (or power) over them; children are sometimes angry at parents, teachers, and bigger or older kids. Adults are often angry at 'the government,' or 'the system.'

If you are fortunate, your parents, teachers, and government treat you justly. They give you some choice about what happens to you, so that you are not helpless. Then you won't become angry at them often. However, you may be angry at yourself occassionally, if you feel helpless to do what you think you should be able to do. You might become angry if you can't hit the ball as far as you think you should, and so on. Usually, if you are like most people, some injustices **will** happen to you, and sometimes you will feel helpless, and you will be angry now and then.

Occassionally many people become angry at once, They feel that something affecting their lives is unjust, and they feel helpless to stop it. The Viet Nam War is a good example. Thousands of people felt it was an unjust war, and that all their protests fell on deaf ears. Since no one, individually, could stop the war, most of the people who protested it felt helpless and angry.

Many people feel the same way about pollution and the desecration of the world environment, about racial and sex discrimination, about unemployment and poverty and taxation in the United States, or about the increase in crime or drug abuse.

Often what one group of people sees as injustice, another group feels is just, or right. Usually the angry group works hard to change what they believe is unjust, while the other group works to keep things the way they are.

What do you think about the issues mentioned above? Would you work to change any of them? Do you feel angry about any of them?

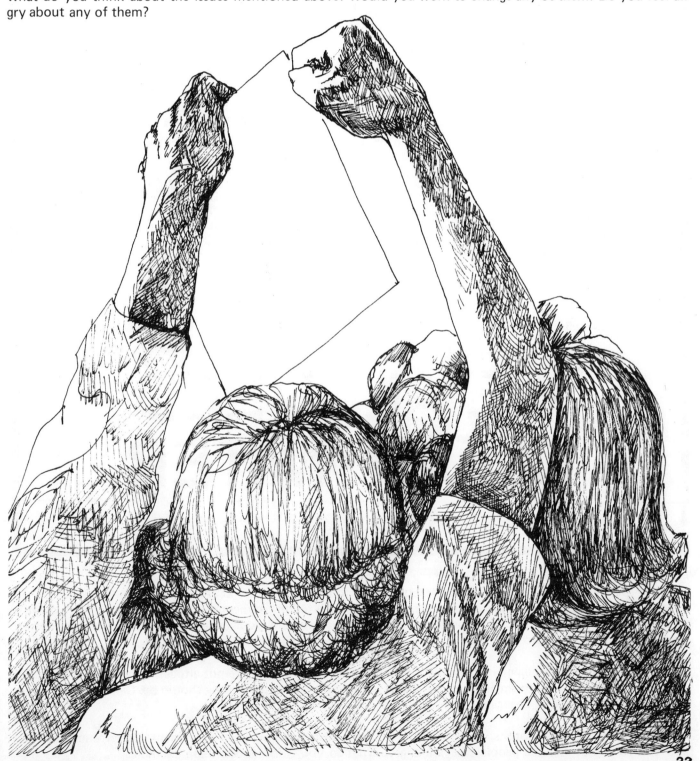

WE ALL NEED CLEAN WATER

When you act in anger, you may do something you would never do in a cool, rational moment. People sometimes kill other people in a rage, when they never would have thought of murder at another time. But most people are in better control of their feelings. You may be angry enough to hurt someone else, but usually you think first. When you do, you may think of a constructive, helpful way to vent your anger, instead of a destructive way. Then you don't hurt yourself or other people, and you may do something really helpful.

Usually, if you can stop being angry long enough, you can see that you are not altogether helpless. You can do something, even if it is very small, to cause things to be more as you think they should be. Can you think of actions people have taken to change what they were angry about?

Think about civil rights protests, peace marches, and the woman's liberation movement. Often, such activities help everyone, not just the people who are angry. What so you think about these examples?

Sharon Cellars
1234 Willow Dr.
Hometown, U.S.A.

My congress
Capital City, U.S.A.

Dear Congressperson:
I am angry. My bike was
stolen. I want it back.

Sincerely,
Shari

What makes you angry? What can you do to change it? If your bike were stolen, or you got a bad grade on a paper you had worked hard on, or if your little brother demolished your 'good stuff,' what could you do to change things, so they wouldn't happen again.

GROUP ACTION

Divide into groups. Let each person in the small group tell what makes him angry, sticking mostly to the personal, such as when a little brother or sister messes up your belongings. Write these down, as a group, to share with everyone later. Now, let each person tell what he does when he is angry. Make a list of these, too. If people haven't talked about why they become angry at school, take another minute or two to talk it over. Let each tell what he does about his anger at school.

Talk about whether the things that make you angry at home are different from those that make you angry at school. Do you find it easier to show anger toward people you care about (like your family) than toward people you're not so sure about (perhaps like kids at school or the teacher? Finally, talk about whether anything can really MAKE you angry. Do you have a choice?

JOURNAL

1. In your journal, quickly write five 'world-wide' events about which you have felt angry.

2. Write five personal happenings that make you angry (things that happen directly to you, not to most people in general.

3. Write what you can do to change any of the ten items you have listed.

4. Write a paragraph about whatever (person or thing) you become angry about most frequently. Tell why you are angry.

FEAR

Fear is the feeling that danger is close by, that something dangerous is about to happen. You might feel it because of something **external**. For example, the wind starts to blow and you hear a tornado warning on the radio or you see a building on fire, an automobile careening out of control, or somebody bigger than you threatens to beat you up.

You know you can hurt. You are afraid, and adrenalin rushes through your body, to help you protect yourself.

Again, you might feel fear because of something **internal.** You get cold and sweaty when you have to speak in front of a group. or when you go to a party where you don't know many people. Maybe you are alone in the dark, or you are doing a new thing for the first time. You don't know exactly what is going to happen, and you feel afraid, even when you know that physical danger is unlikely. But your **feelings** can be hurt.

Both these fears are real, and most people feel them. Yet each person's fears are individual, and so are their ways of reacting to fear. One person might fear high places and react by refusing to get off the ground, while another becomes a sky jumper to overcome his fear. One person will fear speaking in public and never make speeches. Another will react to the same fear by becoming a good speaker and speaking in public every chance he gets. Probably these people are equally afraid, but they react in different ways to control their particular feelings. (If you do nothing, your fear will probably control you).

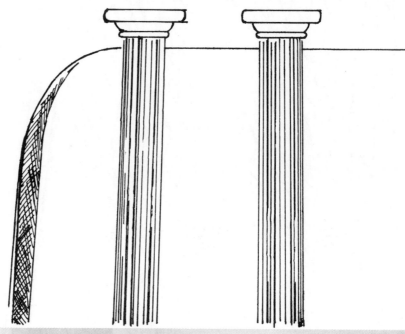

Most people have a combination of both external and internal fears, and each person has his own ways of dealing with these feelings. It is a good idea to know what your fears are, because you can use them to help yourself grow.

Some fears are helpful---as when you run away from a charging bull to keep yourself from being mangled. Other fears help you to develop courage and self-respect. For example, you go ahead and make a speech, meet a new person, or play a new game or sport. Then you see you can do even more than you thought you could, even when you are afraid.

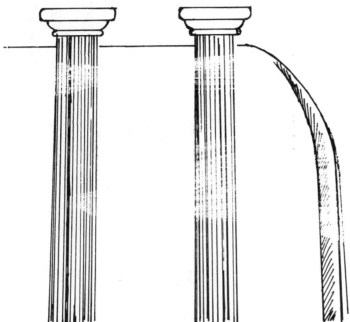

Do not hesitate to admit your fears, for they can give you courage and strength, and often other people can help handle them. The fears that are not helpful are the ones you can't name, or the ones that control you. You just feel nervous and uneasy, as if something bad or dangerous is about to happen, but you don't know exactly why you feel that way. Perhaps you know you fear a particular thing, but you try never to think about it or change your feelings---then you let your fear control you.

"IT IS MORE IMPORTANT TO HAVE COURAGE THAN IT IS TO BE UNAFRAID."

As you get to know more about yourself, you'll start to recognize your fears. You probably will see that some are helpful to you and you will decide to keep or use them. Others, you may want to change, and you may find yourself getting rid of some altogether. Just remember that everyone else is afraid sometimes, too, and that it is more important to have courage than it is to be unafraid. Fear is often wise, and it comes from your instinct to protect yourself and stay alive.

Right now, in your class, look around you. What do these other people fear? Are you afraid of them? Are they afraid of you?

Have you ever made fun of someone for being afraid? Has anyone ever made fun of you for being afraid? Talk together about this. What are some possible reasons a person would make fun of another person, just because he is afraid? Are you ever embarrassed or ashamed of being afraid? Do you talk with anyone when you are afraid?

Has anyone---like a parent or teacher---ever been angry at you for being afraid, or told you that you were a 'big baby' if you did not do a certain thing? Are boys told this more often than girls? Why? Boys have probably been told to 'be a man', But have girls been told to 'be a woman'? What is the difference, and what do you think about it?

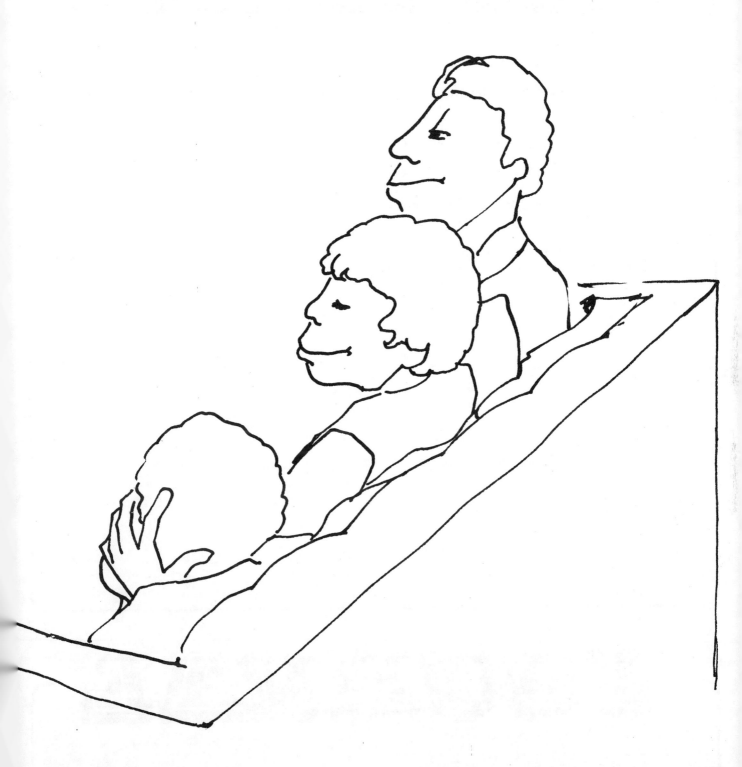

Think for a minute about another kind of fear most people experience: being scared when you know you are safe. For example, you watch a horror movie on T V in your own living room with your parents nearby. Or you hear a ghost story in class at school. That is a delicious fear, isn't it? Your imagination is at work, but you know you are safe.

Fear can be exciting and challenging, if you know---or believe---that you will come out safe. Can you compare this feeling to someone who does a heroic deed, such as saving someone from burning a building, or making a rescue during a flood or a war? Does the hero believe that he is safe? What do you think?

GROUP ACTION

1. Divide into groups and allow each person 3-5 minutes to tell about a scary thing that happened to him.

2. Let each person quickly tell one thing he does when he is afraid.

3. Give each person one or two minutes to talk about scary dreams he has.

4. If you have time, let each group tell ghost stories, or talk about scary movies they have seen. Talk about how this kind of fright affects you.

5. Let each member of the group quickly tell one external thing that scares him, and one internal thing. Can you help each other with these fears?

JOURNAL

In your journal today, write about one frightening dream you have had. Now write a story about the scariest thing that ever happened to you.

HAPPINESS

Perhaps you can define happiness for yourself better than anyone else can, because it is so different to different people. Very small things can make you feel happy. The sun shines when you go on a picnic, someone says you look unusually nice, that you wrote a good paper, or played a good game. You may simply find that most things are going well for you, so you feel happy and that your life is good.

If you are like most people, you are happy or have other 'good' feelings much more often than you have 'bad' feelings or experiences. Yet the 'bad' feelings may stand out more in your mind. Psychological studies show that most people remember pain longer than they remember pleasure! Is that true for you? If you broke your leg and got a new bike, which do you think you would remember longer?

With the whole class, talk about what makes you happy, and make a list on the chalkboard. Talk about what you do when you are happy. Can you think of activities that would make you happier, more often, at school? List these suggestions on the chalkboard.

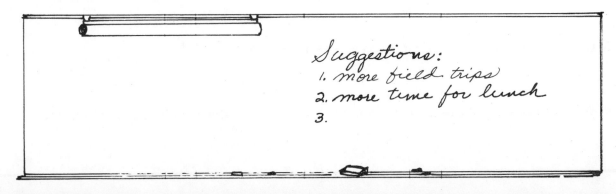

Suggestions:
1. more field trips
2. more time for lunch
3.

GROUP ACTION

1. In small groups, let each person tell one thing that makes him happy. Write these on a sheet of paper to put up later for everyone to see.

2. Remember the book called Happiness is a Warm Puppy? Let each person make one page for such a book. Each can write and illustrate whatever he likes. Then take them all up and staple them into a book.

JOURNAL

1. Quickly write ten things your are happy about right now.

2. Write five things you have done recently that might make other people happy.

3. Quickly write five things you DO when you are happy.

4. Write a story about the best present you ever had or the best Christmas or the best birthday.

JOY

Although you may be happy much of the time, you probably experience joy less frequently. Joy is greater than simple happiness. You feel it when you are truly exhilarated and open to yourself and the world. You feel that you're part of all the world, and that all the world is part of you. Do you ever feel that way?

You might feel joyous when you are zipping down a hill on your bike, when you are swimming in the ocean, watching a sunset or sunrise, or maybe just looking in the mirror! Maybe you feel it when you go beyond 'just being you,' and you become a part of all things. You say, 'I live here, too, on the earth, and that is good---for me and everyone!'

Sometimes your feelings of joy are so private that you don't want to tell them to anyone. Again you may want to tell your feelings to everyone. Sometimes a joyous experience is just something that happens, almost accidentally. Other times it is something you hoped for and planned. Some psychologists call joy a 'peak experience,' a time when your whole self is at a peak. You can probably remember, without thinking very hard, some of your peak experiences.

GROUP ACTION

Let each person in the group tell one thing he would contribute to the world, if he could, that would give him a 'peak' of satisfaction. Whatever individuals think of---breaking a baseball record, being a jazz singer, discovering a cure for cancer, finding a new source of energy, having a good family, making a better space shot---all are acceptable and legitimate. Have each group write its list on paper and share them with everyone, then put them on the wall for people to read again, later.

JOURNAL

Today, write about a time when you felt happier than happy, when you felt joyous, just to be alive. This is your private record, and no one else will read it, unless you give permission.

OTHER FEELINGS

You have many feelings, other than the ones talked about in this book. You have just read and talked about some of the most common feelings, but you may also feel grief over a loss, as when a pet dies, or you lose someone you love. You may feel sad sometimes, or depressed. You may feel frustrated, jealous or mean, or loving, helpful or kind.

You feel all the time, and at almost any given time you can tell what your feelings are---at least you can if you are not too concerned about what other people want you to feel or about what you 'should' feel. Your feelings make you an individual---the special you---but at the same time they make you similar to other people. Nothing makes you richer than genuinely sharing a feeling with another person, but it is also enriching to know, explore, and develop you own private feelings in a constructive way.

JOURNAL
GROUP ACTION

Because there are so many other feelings to be explored, you may want to write more about them in your journal, now. Also, you may want to talk with the whole class, or in small groups, about other feelings you frequently have. Make your own assignments, today, and talk about whatever you like.

We must preserve our natural resources and keep the world clean so that when we children grow up we will have some clean air to breathe and a clean place to live. If we do not use what we have now wisely, by the time we children are grown there will not be anything left for us. I think it is terrible how grown-ups treat the world. They waste water, pour garbage into the lakes and streams, and pile up old cars and junk on the streets of cities. I just hope that there is some air and space to be clean in when I'm grown. I'll bet grown-ups just don't think......

Chapter 7

Actions Speak Louder Than Words
or: What Do You Really Think?

Rusty said he was very interested in stopping pollution and in preserving the natural invironment. He liked to give talks about this, and almost all his projects and research papers at school were on the same subject.

Yet, his locker was a shambles, his belongings were frequently torn up or lost because he threw them around school in any convenient place. At lunch he scattered crumbs and pieces of food, and he often left his lunch bag and sandwich wrappers lying on the floor.

Rusty sincerely thought he wanted to help his environment, but his actions told a different story.

When other people stopped listening to his lectures, Rusty became angry, but he refused to change his ways. What did he really believe? Can anything be done about the situation?

Eva went to the same school as Rusty. She said her favorite activity was the Friday afternoon school dance. At home, she played records everyday and practiced alone, so she knew the latest steps and was a very good dancer. But when she went to the Friday afternoon dances, she folded her arms tight across her chest, thrust her neck forward, and planted her feet firmly apart on the floor. Eva was seldom asked to dance and she wondered why. Could you tell her? Do you think she said one thing while her body said another?

A friend of Eva's told her she didn't look as if she wanted to dance, and at first Eva was very angry. But then she started to think about herself and realized that her friend was right; her shyness was causing her to appear belligerent (as if she wanted to fight) when that was not the way she felt at all. She really did want to dance.

Eva tried hard to relax and concentrate on the music, instead of worrying about feeling shy or nervous. After a couple of weeks, she started to look relaxed. When she was asked to dance and showed how much she enjoyed it, she was very pleased to get some deserved attention as a good dancer.

58

What differences can you see in the way Rusty and Eva behaved? Eva made some important decisions about herself, and changed her actions, so she could do what she valued — dance. Do you think Rusty could do that, too, instead of just being angry when no one listens to him? Would you be angry if a friend told you to 'practice what you preach ?

Both Rusty and Eva were faced with decisions, just as you are, every day. You have so many decisions to make daily, and your opinion is important in so many situations, that it is often hard to know what you believe.

From the time you wake up in the morning until you go to sleep at night, you have decisions to make. Somehow you make them, big ones and small ones —unless, of course, you have somebody else to tell you what to do at all times, or unless you ignore every decision and end up doing whatever is **left** to do, instead of making a choice.

Although making decisions is hard and often frustrating, you probably would rather make up your own mind about what you do as often as you can, instead of having someone else decide for you.

Have you ever found yourself in Rusty's predicament, or Eva's where you **said** one belief and **acted** another? That happens to most people now and then, but if you study your own actions and try to understand what your values really are, it won't happen to you often. How can you do that?

A simple definition of values is whatever is valuable to you. But to understand your values, so you can see how they affect your actions, you need to ask yourself how much you value a particular thing in relation to something else, why you value it, and what you do about it.

For instance, three people may say they value baseball highly. The first values it because he or she plays well and likes the physical action of playing. The second enjoys sitting in the sun and being entertained by an active game. The third always eats several hotdogs at each game, and says the stadium hotdogs are the best in the world. Each person does value baseball, but each is also demonstrating other values (playing, being interntained, eating). Which do you think the third person values more highly, baseball, stadium hotdogs, or eating? If given a choice of going to a baseball game, to the beach, or to a good restaurant, do you think either of these people would choose baseball?

In another situation, the same three people might all ignore baseball if given a choice of whether to contribute a large amount of money toward a new baseball park or toward making a breakthrough in cancer research. You can see that your values may be determined by several things at once, such as what you really like to do, what choices are open, and the possible contribution you will make, for yourself and other people. Your underlying values play a part in most of the decisions you make.

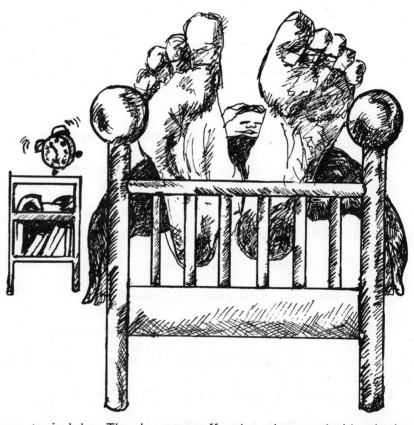

What decisions **do** you make? Think of your typical day. The alarm goes off and you have to decide whether to hop right up or grab a few more minutes sleep. What are you going to wear to school? Do you have time for breakfast or should you quickly finish last night's homework? (If you don't eat, you may feel too hungry to do the work anyway, so what do you do?) Will anyone know if you don't brush your teeth? You probably have even more decisions to make at your home before you go to school, but you get the picture. Decisions, decisions, decisions---they continue throughout the day.

Knowing more about your own values and taking a close look at your actions may make your many decisions easier to handle. Take turns around the room quickly and let each person say one thing he or she values.

GROUP ACTION

Remain with the entire class today, while you show your values by VOTING. As the teacher or leader calls out each item, show how you feel about your values by: waving your hand high if it is very important (or true) for you; raising your hand halfway if it is fairly important; holding your hand down if the item is fairly unimportant (or untrue) to you.

Move rapidly, and don't stop to discuss items until you are finished. Vote on every item and for all parts of items as the leader calls them out.

Items for voting:

1. Ice cream is one of the world's best desserts.

2. I have to get eight hours sleep every night.

3. I think everyone should play at least one sport well.

4. People should always smile and appear friendly when they meet someone new.

5. The school cafeteria food is great!

6. All bombs and nuclear weapons should be banned from the world.

7. If I had a friend with bad breath, I would:
   a. Tell him about it in a kind way
   b. Sneak a bottle of mouthwash into his desk
   c. Say nothing, but try to avoid my friend
   d. Say nothing, do nothing, and hope for the best.

8. I believe people are happier if they stay with their own race.

9. I brush my teeth at least twice a day because:
   a. I want to have healthy teeth and gums
   b. My parents taught me to
   c. I'm afraid no one will like me if I don't
   d. I don't brush my teeth twice a day!

10. I usually choose my own clothes.

11. I will argue, or even fight, for what I believe.

12. At sometime in my life, I have stolen something.

13. I would be angry if someone told me to go away and leave him/her alone.

14. I eat lots of vegetables, every chance I get.

15. I like to work, to earn money.

16. I usually share whatever I have with other people.

17. I hate a sloppy eater!

18. If I saw an old man leaded down with packages trying to open a door, I would:
    a. Open the door because it is good manners
    b. Open the door because he obviously needs help
    c. Let him get in the best way he can; it's not my problem.

19. I want to make good grades.

20. I want to make a lot of money.

21. I want to go to college.

22. I spend my money as soon as I get it.

23. I keep a journal or diary.

24. When I grow up, I'll probably smoke cigarettes.

25. I think people should try as many drugs as they can, before deciding whether drugs are good or bad.

26. I already know what kind of job I want when I grow up.

27. If my country were at war, I would:
    a. Fight, If I had to
    b. Volunteer for fighting or any other service I could give
    c. Not fight under any circumstances.

28. I like school.

28. If, at a dinner party, I spilled my drink, I would:
    a. Leave the table, feeling embarrassed
    b. Quietly ask the hostess or a waiter for help
    c. Cover the mess with my napkin and ignore it.

30. I like learning.

31. I often think of being someone else.

32. Learning about myself means a lot to me.

33. I like me.

After you have voted you might want to talk or write about some of the items (other similar items can be found in books by Sidney Simm.) Another day---with the entire class or in your small groups, rank the items below in the order most important to you, and discuss your reasons. You can have more discussion in small groups, although fewer people will hear each person. You might take more than one day, or class, for this.

1. If I were some kind of star, I would rather be: a great doctor; a movie star; a scientist everyone knows, such as Albert Einstein; a famous writer.

2. If I could make one great contribution to the world, I would like: to discover a cure for cancer; stop all wars; give everyone in the world enough food to keep healthy.

3. If I could have one complete collection I would choose; every bubble gum card, a rock of every kind, every rare monkey.

4. If I were seeing a good friend before he or she moved away, possibly for the last time ever, I would: take him or her to a good restaurant where we could eat and talk; invite him or her to spend the night at my house; give him or her a portable T V; get all our friends together for a party.

5. If I were 87 years old and on my deathbed, I would be happiest to remember that I had: brought up a good family; made so much money I could buy anything I wanted; had always been gracious to other people; had been a good teacher and influenced many young people.

6. If I only took one subject at school, I would take: English, history, art, math, science, physical education.

7. If my father saw me having a fight, I would: hide; ask him to help me beat the kid up; tell him the problem; not do anything until he gave his opinion.

8. If one of these had to happen to me, I would rather: be permanently scarred and disfigured in an accident; live in poverty for my entire life; be unable to finish high school.

9. If I won $100,000 in a contest, I would: give at least half of it to charity; buy a big house for my family; travel around the world; put it in a savings account and spend the interest on myself.

What do you do to show your values?

With the entire class, decide on at least one activity you might do to demonstrate your beliefs. For instance you might write something you feel strongly about. You might stage a clean-up campaign around your school or neighborhood to show how you feel about your environment. You might make posters to put up, illustrating a balanced environment, or some other idea. Discuss what you believe, and decide together what you can do to show others how important your beliefs are to you.

JOURNAL

Make four columns on a sheet of paper in your journal. In the first, write five things you value very highly (people, activities, things---whatever you value most).

In the second column, write WHY you value each of the items in column 1.

In the third column, write what you DO to demonstate your values. Then, in the last column write anything you do that might DENY your real feelings.

Example:

1. I Value	2. Why?	3. I do	4. But sometimes I also
My brother	He's fun to play with. He likes me.	play with him, help him with homework, let him use my games	fight with him, make him do my work, go into his room uninvited.

In your private journal, write a short essay on *This is What I Believe.* Include what you DO about your beliefs.

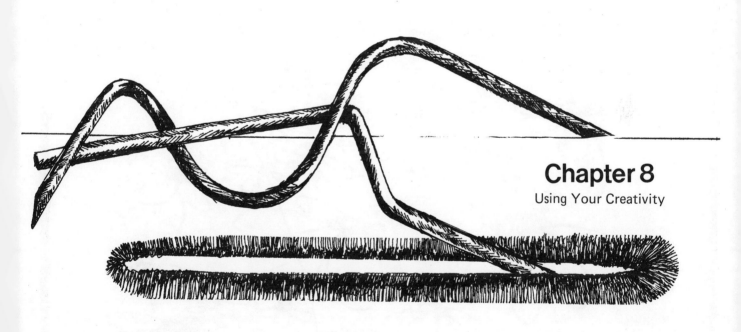

Chapter 8

Using Your Creativity

Marty got up and discovered that his only clean pair of pants had no button at the waist. It was almost time for school, so there was no time to sew on a new button. He didn't want to go around all day with the uncomfortable feeling that he was losing his pants, and he looked for a safety pin. There was none. He did find a paper clip, though, and with a little maneuvering he made it into a fastener to keep his pants together. He used his creativity.

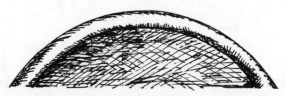

Alice was just finishing the cover for her last book report of the year. She held up her paintbrush to admire what she had done, when suddenly three large red drops of paint splashed onto her picture. At first she was upset, because whe didn't have time to make another cover. Then she looked at the red splashes and decided they looked like flowers, so she added some more splashes and made a whole field of red flowers on one side of her cover. Her teacher gave her a good grade and praised her creative artwork.

Tommy had to do the dishes every night after dinner and he found this very boring. But soon his imagination came to his rescue and discovered doing dishes was the perfect time for thinking. Later on when, he was a successful architect, he was asked what made him so creative. 'Washing dishes as a kid,' he said. 'Every kid should have some dishes to wash!' What Tommy meant was that he had found a regular time to explore his own creativity.

Your creativity is one of the greatest of all your natural talents. You use it every day, usually without thinking much about it. You may even think you are not creative. especially if you think of it as something you do only when you paint a picture or write a poem, Have you ever heard people say, 'I'm not creative.' It's not true. Everyone is creative, just as everyone has intelligence.

Why is your creativity so valuable? Because it can help you out of tight spots, can give you pleasure, and best of all, can help you express your feelings and values in a constructive way.

You have already spent some time talking about your feelings and what you value, and you've talked about what you do to show them. By learning to use your creativity better, you can find more and better ways to express your feelings and values.

Learning to use your creativity will help you focus your energy. When you feel yourself becoming angry, afraid, or frustrated, think of what you can do, or create. With practice, you'll find your actions being constructive or helpful far more often than they hurt or destroy.

Does this sound difficult? If you keep in mind that it is a way of thinking and acting that you already use every-day (instead of thinking that it has to produce a great work of art), you'll find that it is fun as well as helpful. After all, Marty would have felt miserable all day, Alice would have gotten a low grade on her sloppy, paint-spattered report, and Tommy may not have built up the kind of thinking that helped him become a good arch-itect, if they had not used their creativity. They could have felt resentful or angry, and blamed other people for their problems, but they didn't---they created instead. See if you can find some creative ways to avoid problems or situations that usually leave you with negative feelings.

GROUP ACTION

One of the best ways to sharpen your creativity is to practice seeing familiar things in a new way, or from a different point of view. Try this with the activities below by acting them out, or writing and talking about them.

Some of these activities can be done in a few minutes, while others will take a class period or longer. Almost all require some preparation. For example, if you want to try being blind, you'll have to bring blindfolds, or if you want to have a taste test, you'll have to bring food. Read through the activities. Then make plans for the ones you want to do. Many of them are more fun if done more than once.

1. Could you recognize people or find your way around your classroom if you were blind? Take turns being blindfolded, walk around the room or try to identify people by their voices or by touch. Write about how you felt, and the new viewpoints you have.

2. Describe a tiger to an Eskimo who has never seen one, but knows about polar bears. What would you say? Divide into pairs and try it.

3. How many things can you think of that are like an 'o'? Go quickly around the room to get suggestions.

4. Discuss which is friendlier, a kitchen or bedroom? Which is meaner, a rock or a tree? Which is softer, a cloud or the sun? Which is darker, night or sleep? Which is faster, music or dance?

5.   If you had 10 million safety pins, what all could you do with them? Brainstorm for ideas.

6.   Be an animal. Let each person choose an animal and act it out until someone guesses the animal.

7.   Tell what you would think about if you were a goldfish bowl, or a rock, or a tree, or a river. Write about one of these things.

8.   Collect some familiar objects, such as a button, pencil, rock, or whatever you can find. Pass these around and let each person tell one use for them, other than their usual function. Look at objects from a midget's point of view, or a giant's, or an ant's, or in some other way.

9.   Have a taste test. Bring in some food of different textures and let people try to identify them while blindfolded and holding their noses. Write about how you felt.

10. Place an object in the center of the group (chair, hat, etc.) and let several people take turns showing a use for it, without talking (the chair might be used as a driver's seat, then turned over and used as a slide, etc.).

11. Think of 'happy endings' for the following situations. Act them out several different ways, if you like.
     a. Your father spanked you for something you didn't do.
     b. You get all 'F's' on your report card.
     c. Your bike is stolen.
     d. You forgot your bus fare and the bus is coming.
     e. Your best friend asks you to go swimming, but you can't swim.
     f. You are given an award for being the school's best sport and you forget your acceptence speech.
     g. You take two good friends to a party and when you start to introduce them to the hostess, you forget their names.
     h. You forget your homework and leave it home for the third straight day.
     i. You steal a sandwich from someone's lunch and nobody knows who did it, but now the person is hungry.
     j. Someone steals your lunch money.
     k. You are walking home from school when the neighborhood bully hits you with a rock.
     l. Someone does you a big favor and you run away, forgetting to say thanks.
     m. You find you are going to have to stay in bed for a month because of sickness.

12. Put everyone's name in a hat. Draw a name, then make a DESIGN describing the person you drew, (not a drawing of the person) using not more than three colors to finish your description. See if the class can guess each person by the design and colors. Tell why you chose the design and colors you did for your particular person.

13. Let people 'walk' these different ways: walk happy, walk mad, scared, mean, cold, hot, tired, joyful. Let people express these feelings just with their faces.

14. How many things can you think of that you would like to do at school, or on the playground, that you don't do now?

JOURNAL

Look around your classroom and choose some object that is not alive. Now write about you and your class from that object's viewpoint. For instance, what would the pencil sharpener see, think, feel about you and your class?

Chapter 9

More About You

A long time ago, people thought most events were caused by gods. They thought people could affect what happened by making the gods happy or angry. Some believed they had good crops and plenty of food when the gods were pleased with what humans did, and that bad crops and hunger were caused by humans who displeased the gods. If a person had an accident or some bad luck, such as breaking a leg or having the house burn, he or she would look back very carefully, to see what could have made the gods so angry.

There are many ancient stories---called myths--- from all old cultures, which explain why things happened. You may already know some of these stories.

Over the years, scientists have learned about nature, how people work, and the causes of diseases. We now know these things are not caused by gods. Yet we've also learned that some things that happen to individual people are caused by the people themselves. And now we have a science called psychology—the study of the human mind and human behavior—which helps us understand more about how this happens.

Compared to most other sciences, such as earth science, astrology, chemistry, physics, and medicine, psychology is still new. Because people change so much, and they are so different from one another, psychologists have fewer 'facts' to work with than most scientists, and they have a difficult job.

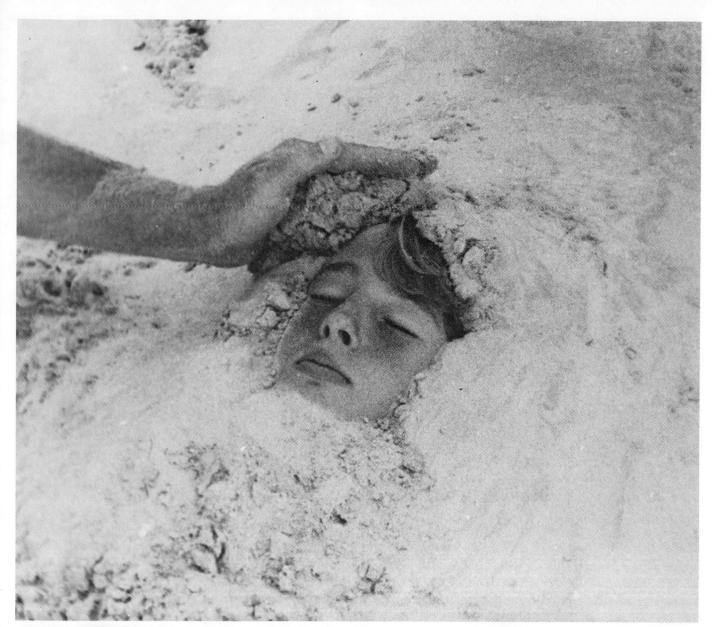

When psychologists study people, they learn some of the things you have studied in this book. They learn about the people's customs and manners, about their feelings and values, and they make case histories. Then they know about the people's childhood and what is going on in their lives. From all this information, they try to understand why people behave as they do, what motivates them. If you know why you do the things you do, it may be easier to change any of your behavior that you don't like or any that is not helpful.

MODELING — Psychologists know now that one of the earliest ways people learn is by modeling behavior after other people they see. This means you try to do what you see other people do. At first, you usually model after your mother or father, or some other person who takes care of you. They laugh, and you laugh back. They clap their hands to play patty-cake, and you clap your hands, too. They cuddle you, and you cuddle back, or you cuddle your stuffed animal, doll, or other toys.

Later, when you can walk, you follow them around, trying to do what they are doing. If your mother sweeps the floor, you make sweeping motions, too. You don't know she is trying to get the floor clean, you just 'sweep.' Your mother's behavior is **motivated** (she is cleaning the floor) while yours is **imitative**. If you have a motive, it is to be like your mama, not to get the floor clean.

76

To adults, children's early modeling is often funny, because they see the child does not understand the motivation behind the behavior he or she imitates. Can you remember doing anything when you were very young that adults laughed about? Why not take some time to remember and talk about this.

As you grow older, more people come into your life, and you imitate them, too. Little children spend hours playing grown-up. They dress up in other people's clothes, and imitate the actions they see.

Imitating, or modeling, continues throughout your life, but after awhile you become selective and you choose only the people or behavior that appeals to you. You may learn to jump rope or throw a baseball by imitating someone, or you may learn a particular way of laughing, walking or talking by watching and listening to someone you admire. Has anyone ever told you that you walk (or anything else) just like your grandfather, an aunt, or somebody else?

While you model some of your behavior after other people, someone else may be modeling after you. That is one of the ways people influence one another. Do you have a younger friend or relative who thinks you are great and who tries to 'be like' you? Have you ever taught any of your friends at school something you are particularly good at by **showing** them how to do it?

By modeling, you learn much of your behavior that you want to keep, but you can also learn behavior that you later want to change. If your parents yell at you a lot, you may find yourself yelling at other people. Or, you may decide that you don't want to 'be like' that, and become determined not to yell. You can see how important it is to have 'good models' around you, but you can also see how hard it is to **be** a good model. Have you ever been told that someone else was a 'bad influence' on you? Why would someone say that? Do you think you are a 'pretty good model' for a younger child?

GROUP ACTION

Divide into small groups and let each person:

1. Tell who he or she would most like to be if not themselves. Why?

2. Tell one thing about his or her mother or father they would like to 'be like.'

3. Tell one way the teacher provides 'a good model.'

4. Tell one way that each member in the group is 'a good model,' or has an admirable characteristic

    1. John listens when you talk to him.
    2. Erica is a good softball pitcher.

5. Tell about someone who was a 'hero' to him or her when they were very young. Why?

JOURNAL

From the people you know, think of an adult you would like to be like when you grow up. Write what you like about him or her, and why you admire the person.

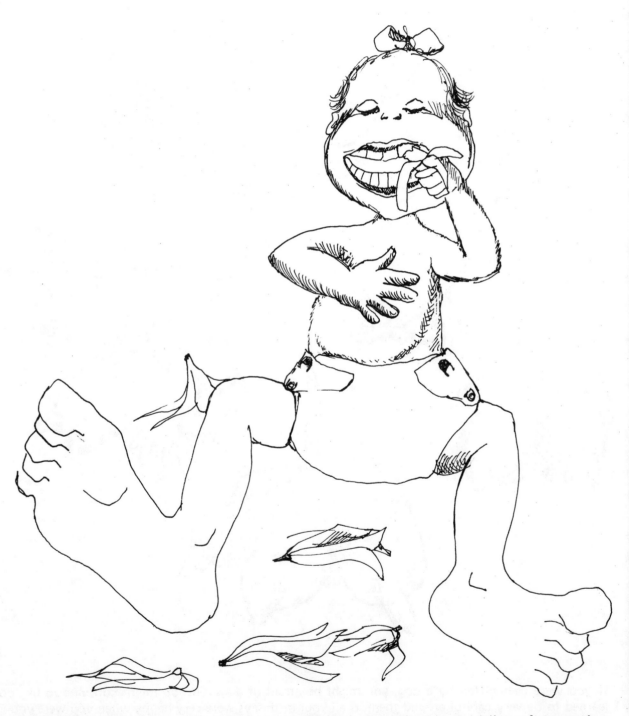

Other Reasons You Behave As You Do — Not all of your behavior is determined by modeling, of course. Any of the millions of things that have happened in your life can influence the way you act, or feel, at some time. If you ever become ill from eating bananas as a baby, you might dislike bananas for the rest of your life. Or you might continue to like bananas, but have learned not to eat too many.

If you were ever bitten by a dog, you might be afraid of dogs. Or you might continue to like dogs, but have learned to be very careful around them. If all your birthdays were very happy when you were young, you might always look forward to birthdays as a special time. Or later, as an adult, you may hate them because they are no longer as happy as when you were a child. Also, you might learn to like or want something that is not good for you, as in the case of a few people who 'like to be sick' because everyone is nicer to them then than at any other time. People learn different facts and ways of behaving from all that happens to them.

Many psychologists believe that everything in your life is still stored somewhere in your complex intelligence system, even if you don't remember it all at once, or even know that it is there. Some of it is in your conscious--- that is you remember it anytime you want, and you know it is there. Some of it is in your unconscious. This you have to work hard to recall, although parts of it may sometimes just appear, as when you suddenly feel you've been in a place before, or a smell, sound, or something you see brings up a memory you thought you had 'forgotten.' In a way, you are like a complicated computer, storing up all the information 'fed into you.' But since you have feelings, and a brain, you sometimes have to do more that press a button---as you would with a computer---to recall your information. But any of this information, whether you remember it consciously or not, can influence the way you behave, or act.

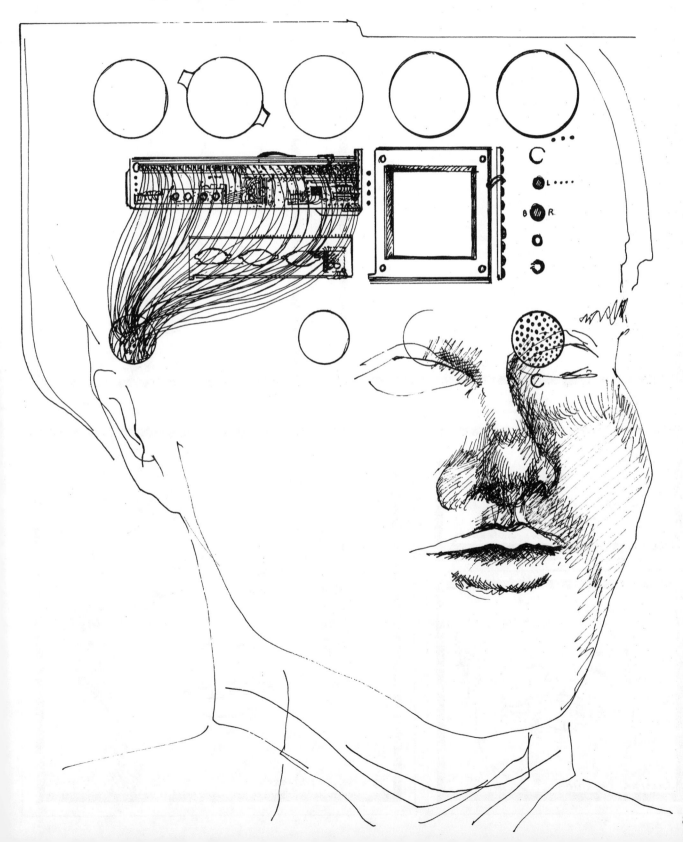

With your class, remember when you were very young. Do you know how much you weighed when you were born, and how long you were? Most babies weigh 6-8 pounds and are 19-21 inches long. Look at you now! Haven't you changed!

George 8 lbs. 6 oz.-20"

George 2 years

George - sleeping

George - laughing

George 12 years

Talk about some of the things that have happened to you, and the ways you've changed. Can you remember what you liked to play and who your friends were when you were two years old? Did you have a favorite pet or toy then? What is your very first memory? Can you remember going to sleep then, or being left alone? Can you remember getting something you wanted very much? That was it? Do you ever feel you've been in a place before when you know you haven't? Can you think of any reasons for this?

JOURNAL
GROUP ACTION

List five things that you think you will always remember. Have they influenced the way you are? (These might be such things as The time I broke my leg, When I got my first bike, When my sister (brother) was born, etc.)

Now write about some of your memories, good and bad, from the time you first remember, up to now.

Chapter 10

You And Other People

By now, you've probably become a pretty good detective, where people are concerned. You've gathered a lot of information about yourself and other people, and you've explored ways to use your knowledge and talents. You've seen how you are like other people in many ways and how you differ from them in your own unique way. Of course, there is much more to know, for it is unlikely that you can ever know a person completely, even if that person is you.

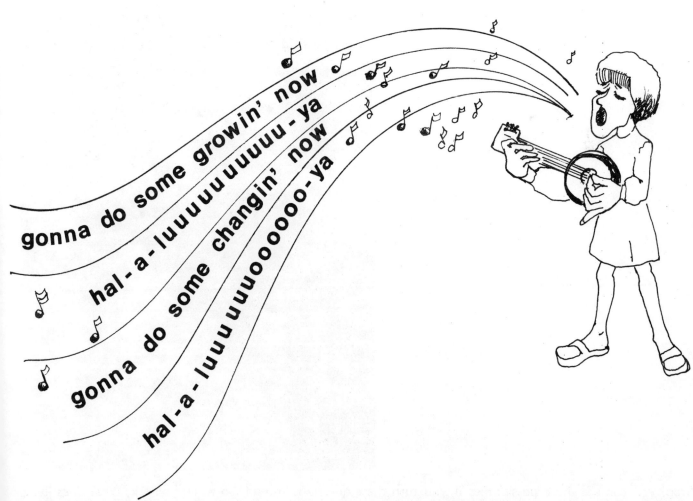

Along the way, you may have started asking some hard questions, such as, What does living mean, to me? Or, How would I like the world to be? As soon as you are mature enough to think---really think---about such questions, you will start trying to find answers, and your own answers will probably grow and change as you do.

Often, you can see more possibilities if you turn these questions around. So when you ask, What does living mean, to me? turn the question around and ask, What does life mean, to other people? And, How would I like the world to be? By considering two sides of these questions, you may see that while you can expect to **get** much for yourself during your lifetime, you also have a responsibility, or expectation to **give** much.

Many of the survivors of concentration camps and war prisons have later said the only way they were able to keep living was to remember that the people who cared for them wanted them to live and return. They were, in effect, living their lives for the people who loved them.

Not many people have to make such extreme sacrifices, but most people do give some of themselves to others, just because the other people care for them. When you remember that you are the only person in the world who is uniquely you, and that some other people know and appreciate your specialness, you can see that the world truly will suffer a loss if you do not share yourself and become all you can.

How do you think the world is going to change, as you grow up? Can you think of ways that you, as an individual, can make this a better place to live?

GROUP ACTION

Divide into small groups and have a brainstorming session about what the world will be like in ten years. Bring up any ideas you have, and write them in a list to share with the class. Later, put up the lists, so everyone can read them again.

Next, in your group, plan an 'ideal' world. Pretend you are on a remote island. You and your group are the only people there, although you can import people one at a time, as you need or want them. What will be in your world, and how will it work? Draw a large picture of your island, showing everything in it. Write a short description of how your society works. Put these around the walls, for everyone to share and question. Be sure that each person in your group agrees with everything you include in your world.

JOURNAL

1. In your jounral, write one question that is very important to you, right now. Then, reverse the question and write it another way. Do your best to answer both questions, in writing.

2. Write a short essay about yourself ten years from now. Where will you be, what will you be doing, and what will you be like?

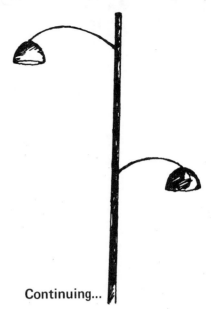

Continuing...

Perhaps you've had a few surprises about yourself or others while using this book, or maybe you learned more about what you think and what you can do. You've started keeping a private journal, so you have a valuable record of yourself at one particular time in your life. Perhaps you'll keep adding to your journal (or perhaps you'll save for your grandchildren!)

You may want to do some of the activities you've tried again, in school or at home. Whatever you do, you have already opened the door to knowing yourself a little wider. If you continue what you've started, keeping your mind open and your creativity sharp, you will undoubtedly find the world becoming a better place for you to live. Like everyone else who studies him or herself, you can look with understanding at the world, and say, 'I live here, too,' with pride and humility, understanding and care, and a sense of the adventurous pioneer. Good luck.